I0473135

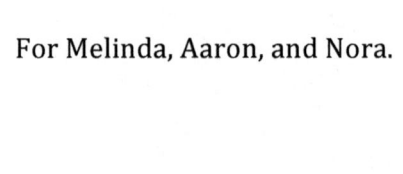

For Melinda, Aaron, and Nora.

Contents

About

The aim of this document is to get you started with developing applications for Node.js, teaching you everything you need to know about "advanced" JavaScript along the way. It goes way beyond your typical "Hello World" tutorial.

Status

You are reading the final version of this book, i.e., updates are only done to correct errors or to reflect changes in new versions of Node.js.

The code samples in this book are tested to work with Node.js version 0.4.9.

Intended audience

This document will probably fit best for readers that have a background similar to my own: experienced with at least one object-oriented language like Ruby, Python, PHP or Java, only little experience with JavaScript, and completely new to Node.js.

Aiming at developers that already have experience with other programming languages means that this document won't cover really basic stuff like data types, variables, control structures and the likes. You already need to know about these to understand this document.

However, because functions and objects in JavaScript are different from their counterparts in most other languages, these will be explained in more detail.

Structure of this document

Upon finishing this document, you will have created a complete web application which allows the users of this application to view web pages and upload files.

Which, of course, is not exactly world-changing, but we will go some extra miles and not only create the code that is "just enough" to make these use cases possible, but create a simple, yet complete framework to cleanly separate the different aspects of our application. You will see what I mean in a minute.

We will start with looking at how JavaScript development in Node.js is different from JavaScript development in a browser.

Next, we will stay with the good old tradition of writing a "Hello World" application, which is a most basic Node.js application that "does" something.

Then, we will discuss what kind of "real" application we want to build, dissect the different parts which need to be implemented to assemble this application, and start working on each of these parts step-by-step.

As promised, along the way we will learn about some of the more advanced concepts of JavaScript, how to make use of them, and look at why it makes sense to use these concepts instead of those we know from other programming languages.

JavaScript and Node.js

JavaScript and You

Before we talk about all the technical stuff, let's take a moment and talk about you and your relationship with JavaScript. This chapter is here to allow you to estimate if reading this document any further makes sense for you.

If you are like me, you started with HTML "development" long ago, by writing HTML documents. You came along this funny thing called JavaScript, but you only used it in a very basic way, adding interactivity to your web pages every now and then.

What you really wanted was "the real thing", you wanted to know how to build complex web sites - you learned a programming language like PHP, Ruby, Java, and started writing "backend" code.

Nevertheless, you kept an eye on JavaScript, you saw that with the introduction of jQuery, Prototype and the likes, things got more advanced in JavaScript land, and that this language really was about more than *window.open()*.

However, this was all still frontend stuff, and although it was nice to have jQuery at your disposal whenever you felt like spicing up a web page, at the end of the day you were, at best, a JavaScript *user*, but not a JavaScript *developer*.

And then came Node.js. JavaScript on the server, how cool is that?

You decided that it's about time to check out the old, new JavaScript. But wait, writing Node.js applications is the one thing; understanding why they need to be written the way they are written means - understanding JavaScript. And this time for real.

Here is the problem: Because JavaScript really lives two, maybe even three lives (the funny little DHMTL helper from the mid-90's, the more serious frontend stuff like jQuery and the likes, and now server-side), it's not that easy to find information that helps you to learn

3

JavaScript the "right" way, in order to write Node.js applications in a fashion that makes you feel you are not just using JavaScript, you are actually developing it.

Because that's the catch: you already are an experienced developer, you don't want to learn a new technique by just hacking around and mis-using it; you want to be sure that you are approaching it from the right angle.

There is, of course, excellent documentation out there. But documentation alone sometimes isn't enough. What is needed is guidance.

My goal is to provide a guide for you.

A word of warning

There are some really excellent JavaScript people out there. I'm not one of them.

I'm really just the guy I talked about in the previous paragraph. I know a thing or two about developing backend web applications, but I'm still new to "real" JavaScript and still new to Node.js. I learned some of the more advanced aspects of JavaScript just recently. I'm not experienced.

Which is why this is no "from novice to expert" book. It's more like "from novice to advanced novice".

If I don't fail, then this will be the kind of document I wish I had when starting with Node.js.

Server-side JavaScript

The first incarnations of JavaScript lived in browsers. But this is just the context. It defines what you can do with the language, but it doesn't say much about what the language itself can do. JavaScript is a "complete" language: you can use it in many contexts and achieve everything with it you can achieve with any other "complete" language.

Node.js really is just another context: it allows you to run JavaScript code in the backend, outside a browser.

In order to execute the JavaScript you intend to run in the backend, it needs to be interpreted and, well, executed. This is what Node.js does, by making use of Google's V8 VM, the same runtime environment for JavaScript that Google Chrome uses.

Plus, Node.js ships with a lot of useful modules, so you don't have to write everything from scratch, like for example something that outputs a string on the console.

Thus, Node.js is really two things: a runtime environment and a library.

In order to make use of these, you need to install Node.js. Instead of repeating the process here, I kindly ask you to visit the official installation instructions[1]. Please come back once you are up and running.

"Hello World"

Ok, let's just jump in the cold water and write our first Node.js application: "Hello World".

Open your favorite editor and create a file called *helloworld.js*. We

---

[1] https://github.com/joyent/node/wiki/Installation

want it to write "Hello World" to STDOUT, and here is the code needed to do that:

```
console.log("Hello World");
```

Save the file, and execute it through Node.js:

```
node helloworld.js
```

This should output *Hello World* on your terminal.

Ok, this stuff is boring, right? Let's write some real stuff.

A full blown web application with Node.js

The use cases

Let's keep it simple, but realistic:

- The user should be able to use our application with a web browser

- The user should see a welcome page when requesting http://*domain*/start which displays a file upload form

- By choosing an image file to upload and submitting the form, this image should then be uploaded to http://*domain*/upload, where it is displayed once the upload is finished

Fair enough. Now, you could achieve this goal by googling and hacking together *something*. But that's not what we want to do here.

Furthermore, we don't want to write only the most basic code to achieve the goal, however elegant and correct this code might be. We will intentionally add more abstraction than necessary in order to get a feeling for building more complex Node.js applications.

The application stack

Let's dissect our application. Which parts need to be implemented in order to fulfill the use cases?

- We want to serve web pages, therefore we need an **HTTP server**

7

- Our server will need to answer differently to requests, depending on which URL the request was asking for, thus we need some kind of **router** in order to map requests to request handlers

- To fullfill the requests that arrived at the server and have been routed using the router, we need actual **request handlers**

- The router probably should also treat any incoming POST data and give it to the request handlers in a convenient form, thus we need **request data handling**

- We not only want to handle requests for URLs, we also want to display content when these URLs are requested, which means we need some kind of **view logic** the request handlers can use in order to send content to the user's browser

- Last but not least, the user will be able to upload images, so we are going to need some kind of **upload handling** which takes care of the details

Let's think a moment about how we would build this stack with PHP. It's not exactly a secret that the typical setup would be an Apache HTTP server with mod_php5 installed. Which in turn means that the whole "we need to be able to serve web pages and receive HTTP requests" stuff doesn't happen within PHP itself.

Well, with node, things are a bit different. Because with Node.js, we not only implement our application, we also implement the whole HTTP server. In fact, our web application and its web server are basically the same.

This might sound like a lot of work, but we will see in a moment that with Node.js, it's not.

Let's just start at the beginning and implement the first part of our stack, the HTTP server.

Building the application stack

A basic HTTP server

When I arrived at the point where I wanted to start with my first "real" Node.js application, I wondered not only how to actually code it, but also how to organize my code. Do I need to have everything in one file? Most tutorials on the web that teach you how to write a basic HTTP server in Node.js have all the logic in one place. What if I want to make sure that my code stays readable the more stuff I implement?

Turns out, it's relatively easy to keep the different concerns of your code separated, by putting them in modules.

This allows you to have a clean main file, which you execute with Node.js, and clean modules that can be used by the main file and among each other.

So, let's create a main file which we use to start our application, and a module file where our HTTP server code lives.

My impression is that it's more or less a standard to name your main file *index.js*. It makes sense to put our server module into a file named *server.js*.

Let's start with the server module. Create the file *server.js* in the root directory of your project, and fill it with the following code:

```
var http = require("http");

http.createServer(function(request, response) {
  response.writeHead(200, {"Content-Type": "text/plain"});
  response.write("Hello World");
  response.end();
}).listen(8888);
```

That's it! You just wrote a working HTTP server. Let's prove it by running and testing it. First, execute your script with Node.js:

```
node server.js
```

Now, open your browser and point it at http://localhost:8888/[1]. This should display a web page that says "Hello World".

That's quite interesting, isn't it. How about talking about what's going on here and leaving the question of how to organize our project for later? I promise we'll get back to it.

Analyzing our HTTP server

Well, then, let's analyze what's actually going on here.

The first line *require*s the *http* module that ships with Node.js and makes it accessible through the variable *http*.

We then call one of the functions the http module offers: *createServer*. This function returns an object, and this object has a method named *listen*, and takes a numeric value which indicates the port number our HTTP server is going to listen on.

Please ignore for a second the function definition that follows the opening bracket of *http.createServer*.

We could have written the code that starts our server and makes it listen at port 8888 like this:

```
var http = require("http");

var server = http.createServer();
server.listen(8888);
```

That would start an HTTP server listening at port 8888 and doing nothing else (not even answering any incoming requests).

---

[1] http://localhost:8888/

The really interesting (and, if your background is a more conservative language like PHP, odd looking) part is the function definition right there where you would expect the first parameter of the *createServer( )* call.

Turns out, this function definition IS the first (and only) parameter we are giving to the *createServer( )* call. Because in JavaScript, functions can be passed around like any other value.

Passing functions around

You can, for example, do something like this:

```
function say(word) {
  console.log(word);
}

function execute(someFunction, value) {
  someFunction(value);
}

execute(say, "Hello");
```

Read this carefully! What we are doing here is, we pass the function *say* as the first parameter to the *execute* function. Not the return value of *say*, but *say* itself!

Thus, *say* becomes the local variable *someFunction* within *execute*, and execute can call the function in this variable by issuing *someFunction( )* (adding brackets).

Of course, because *say* takes one parameter, *execute* can pass such a parameter when calling *someFunction*.

We can, as we just did, pass a function as a parameter to another function by its name. But we don't have to take this indirection of first defining, then passing it - we can define and pass a function as a parameter to another function in-place:

```
function execute(someFunction, value) {
  someFunction(value);
}

execute(function(word){ console.log(word) }, "Hello");
```

We define the function we want to pass to *execute* right there at the place where *execute* expects its first parameter.

This way, we don't even need to give the function a name, which is why this is called an *anonymous function*.

This is a first glimpse at what I like to call "advanced" JavaScript, but let's take it step by step. For now, let's just accept that in JavaScript, we can pass a function as a parameter when calling another function. We can do this by assigning our function to a variable, which we then pass, or by defining the function to pass in-place.

How function passing makes our HTTP server work

With this knowledge, let's get back to our minimalistic HTTP server:

```
var http = require("http");

http.createServer(function(request, response) {
  response.writeHead(200, {"Content-Type": "text/plain"});
```

```
    response.write("Hello World");
    response.end();
}).listen(8888);
```

By now it should be clear what we are actually doing here: we pass the *createServer* function an anonymous function.

We could achieve the same by refactoring our code to:

```
var http = require("http");

function onRequest(request, response) {
    response.writeHead(200, {"Content-Type": "text/plain"});
    response.write("Hello World");
    response.end();
}

http.createServer(onRequest).listen(8888);
```

Maybe now is a good moment to ask: Why are we doing it that way?

Event-driven callbacks

The answer is a) not that easy to give (at least for me), and b) lies in the very nature of how Node.js works. It's event-driven, which is the reason why it's so fast.

You might want to take the time to read Felix Geisendoerfer's excellent post Understanding node.js[2] for some background explanation.

It all boils down to the fact that Node.js works event-driven. Oh and yes, I, too, don't know exactly what that means. But I will try and

---

[2]http://debuggable.com/posts/understanding-node-js:4bd98440-45e4-4a9a-8ef7-0f7ecbdd56cb

explain, why this makes sense for us who want to write web based applications in Node.js.

When we call the *http.createServer* method, we of course not only want to have a server listening at some port, we also want to do something when there is an HTTP request to this server.

The problem is, this happens asynchronously: it happens at any given time, but we only have a single process in which our server runs.

When writing PHP applications, we aren't bothered by this at all: whenever there is an incoming HTTP request, the webserver (usually Apache) forks a new process for just this request, and starts the according PHP script from scratch, which is then executed from top to bottom.

So in regards of control flow, we are in the midst of our Node.js program when a new request arrives at port 8888 - how to handle this without going insane?

Well, this is where the event-driven design of Node.js/JavaScript actually helps, although we need to learn some new concepts in order to master it. Let's see how these concepts are applied in our server code.

We create the server, and pass a function to the method creating it. Whenever our server receives a request, the function we passed will be called.

We don't know when this is going to happen, but we now have a place where we can handle an incoming request. It's our passed function, no matter if we first defined it or passed it anonymously.

This concept is called a *callback*. We pass into some method a function, and the method uses this function to *call back* if an event related to the method occurs.

At least for me, this took some time to understand. Just read Felix' blog post again if you are still unsure.

Let's play around a bit with this new concept. Can we prove that our code continues after creating the server, even if no HTTP request happened and the callback function we passed isn't called? Let's try it:

```
var http = require("http");

function onRequest(request, response) {
  console.log("Request received.");
  response.writeHead(200, {"Content-Type": "text/plain"});
  response.write("Hello World");
  response.end();
}

http.createServer(onRequest).listen(8888);

console.log("Server has started.");
```

Note that I use *console.log* to output a text whenever the *onRequest* function (our callback) is triggered, and another text right *after* starting the HTTP server.

When we start this (*node server.js*, as always), it will immediately output "Server has started." on the command line. Whenever we request our server (by opening http://localhost:8888/[3] in our browser), the message "Request received." is printed on the command line.

Event-driven asynchronous server-side JavaScript with callbacks in action :-)

(Note that our server will probably write "Request received." to STD-OUT two times upon opening the page in a browser. That's because most browser will try to load the favicon by requesting http://localhost:8888/favicon.ico whenever you open http://localhost:8888/).

---

[3]http://localhost:8888/

How our server handles requests

Ok, let's quickly analyze the rest of our server code, that is, the body of our callback function *onRequest( )*.

When the callback fires and our *onRequest( )* function gets triggered, two parameters are passed into it: *request* and *response*.

Those are objects, and you can use their methods to handle the details of the HTTP request that occured and to respond to the request (i.e., to actually send something over the wire back to the browser that requested your server).

And our code does just that: Whenever a request is received, it uses the *response.writeHead( )* function to send an HTTP status 200 and content-type in the HTTP response header, and the *response.write( )* function to send the text "Hello World" in the HTTP response body.

At last, we call *response.end( )* to actually finish our response.

At this point, we don't care for the details of the request, which is why we don't use the *request* object at all.

Finding a place for our server module

Ok, I promised we will get back to how to organize our application. We have the code for a very basic HTTP server in the file *server.js*, and I mentioned that it's common to have a main file called *index.js* which is used to bootstrap and start our application by making use of the other modules of the application (like the HTTP server module that lives in *server.js*).

Let's talk about how to make server.js a real Node.js module that can be used by our yet-to-be-written *index.js* main file.

As you may have noticed, we already used modules in our code, like this:

```
var http = require("http");
```

```
...
```

```
http.createServer(...);
```

Somewhere within Node.js lives a module called "http", and we can make use of it in our own code by requiring it and assigning the result of the require to a local variable.

This makes our local variable an object that carries all the public methods the *http* module provides.

It's common practice to choose the name of the module for the name of the local variable, but we are free to choose whatever we like:

```
var foo = require("http");
```

```
...
```

```
foo.createServer(...);
```

Fine, it's clear how to make use of internal Node.js modules. How do we create our own modules, and how do we use them?

Let's find out by turning our *server.js* script into a real module.

Turns out, we don't have to change that much. Making some code a module means we need to *export* those parts of its functionality that we want to provide to scripts that require our module.

For now, the functionality our HTTP server needs to export is simple: scripts requiring our server module simply need to start the server.

To make this possible, we will put our server code into a function named *start*, and we will export this function:

```
var http = require("http");

function start() {
  function onRequest(request, response) {
    console.log("Request received.");
    response.writeHead(200, {"Content-Type": "text/plain"});
    response.write("Hello World");
    response.end();
  }

  http.createServer(onRequest).listen(8888);
  console.log("Server has started.");
}

exports.start = start;
```

This way, we can now create our main file *index.js*, and start our HTTP there, although the code for the server is still in our *server.js* file.

Create a file *index.js* with the following content:

```
var server = require("./server");

server.start();
```

As you can see, we can use our server module just like any internal module: by requiring its file and assigning it to a variable, its exported functions become available to us.

That's it. We can now start our app via our main script, and it still does exactly the same:

```
node index.js
```

Great, we now can put the different parts of our application into different files and wire them together by making them modules.

We still have only the very first part of our application in place: we can receive HTTP requests. But we need to do something with them - depending on which URL the browser requested from our server, we need to react differently.

For a very simple application, you could do this directly within the callback function *onRequest()*. But as I said, let's add a bit more abstraction in order to make our example application a bit more interesting.

Making different HTTP requests point at different parts of our code is called "routing" - well, then, let's create a module called *router*.

What's needed to "route" requests?

We need to be able to feed the requested URL and possible additional GET and POST parameters into our router, and based on these the router then needs to be able to decide which code to execute (this "code to execute" is the third part of our application: a collection of request handlers that do the actual work when a request is received).

So, we need to look into the HTTP requests and extract the requested URL as well as the GET/POST parameters from them. It could be argued if that should be part of the router or part of the server (or even a module of its own), but let's just agree on making it part of our HTTP server for now.

All the information we need is available through the *request* object which is passed as the first parameter to our callback function *onRequest()*. But to interpret this information, we need some additional Node.js modules, namely *url* and *querystring*.

The *url* module provides methods which allow us to extract the different parts of a URL (like e.g. the requested path and query string), and *querystring* can in turn be used to parse the query string for request parameters:

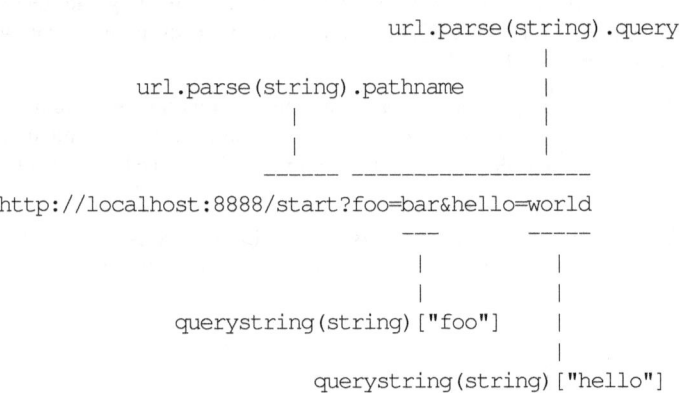

We can, of course, also use *querystring* to parse the body of a POST request for parameters, as we will see later.

Let's now add to our *onRequest()* function the logic needed to find out which URL path the browser requested:

```
var http = require("http");
var url = require("url");

function start() {
  function onRequest(request, response) {
        var pathname = url.parse(request.url).pathname;
        console.log("Request for " + pathname + " received.");
        response.writeHead(200, {"Content-Type": "text/plain"});
        response.write("Hello World");
        response.end();
  }
```

```
  http.createServer(onRequest).listen(8888);
  console.log("Server has started.");
}

exports.start = start;
```

Fine. Our application can now distinguish requests based on the URL path requested - this allows us to map requests to our request handlers based on the URL path using our (yet to be written) router.

In the context of our application, it simply means that we will be able to have requests for the */start* and */upload* URLs handled by different parts of our code. We will see how everything fits together soon.

Ok, it's time to actually write our router. Create a new file called *router.js*, with the following content:

```
function route(pathname) {
  console.log("About to route a request for " + pathname);
}

exports.route = route;
```

Of course, this code basically does nothing, but that's ok for now. Let's first see how to wire together this router with our server before putting more logic into the router.

Our HTTP server needs to know about and make use of our router. We could hard-wire this dependency into the server, but because we learned the hard way from our experience with other programming languages, we are going to loosely couple server and router by injecting this dependency (you may want to read Martin Fowlers excellent post on Dependency Injection[4] for background information).

---

[4]http://martinfowler.com/articles/injection.html

Let's first extend our server's *start()* function in order to enable us to pass the route function to be used by parameter:

```javascript
var http = require("http");
var url = require("url");

function start(route) {
  function onRequest(request, response) {
    var pathname = url.parse(request.url).pathname;
    console.log("Request for " + pathname + " received.");

    route(pathname);

    response.writeHead(200, {"Content-Type": "text/plain"});
    response.write("Hello World");
    response.end();
  }

  http.createServer(onRequest).listen(8888);
  console.log("Server has started.");
}

exports.start = start;
```

And let's extend our *index.js* accordingly, that is, injecting the route function of our router into the server:

```javascript
var server = require("./server");
var router = require("./router");

server.start(router.route);
```

Again, we are passing a function, which by now isn't any news for us.

If we start our application now (*node index.js, as always*), and request an URL, you can now see from the application's output that our HTTP server makes use of our router and passes it the requested pathname:

```
bash$ node index.js
Request for /foo received.
About to route a request for /foo
```

(I omitted the rather annoying output for the /favicon.ico request).

Execution in the kingdom of verbs

May I once again stray away for a while and talk about functional programming again?

Passing functions is not only a technical consideration. With regard to software design, it's almost philosophical. Just think about it: in our index file, we could have passed the *router* object into the server, and the server could have called this object's *route* function.

This way, we would have passed a *thing*, and the server would have used this thing to *do* something. Hey, router thing, could you please route this for me?

But the server doesn't need the thing. It only needs to get something *done*, and to get something done, you don't need things at all, you need *actions*. You don't need *nouns*, you need *verbs*.

Understanding the fundamental mind-shift that's at the core of this idea is what made me really understand functional programming.

And I did understand it when reading Steve Yegge's masterpiece Execution in the Kingdom of Nouns[5]. Go read it now, really. It's one of the best writings related to software I ever had the pleasure to encounter.

---

[5] http://steve-yegge.blogspot.com/2006/03/execution-in-kingdom-of-nouns.html

Routing to real request handlers

Back to business. Our HTTP server and our request router are now best friends and talk to each other as we intended.

Of course, that's not enough. "Routing" means, we want to handle requests to different URLs differently. We would like to have the "business logic" for requests to */start* handled in another function than requests to */upload*.

Right now, the routing "ends" in the router, and the router is not the place to actually "do" something with the requests, because that wouldn't scale well once our application becomes more complex.

Let's call these functions, where requests are routed to, *request handlers*. And let's tackle those next, because unless we have these in place there isn't much sense in doing anything with the router for now.

New application part, new module - no surprise here. Let's create a module called requestHandlers, add a placeholder function for every request handler, and export these as methods of the module:

```
function start() {
  console.log("Request handler 'start' was called.");
}

function upload() {
  console.log("Request handler 'upload' was called.");
}

exports.start = start;
exports.upload = upload;
```

This allows us to wire the request handlers into the router, giving our router something to route to.

At this point we need to make a decision: do we hard-code usage of the requestHandlers module into the router, or do we want a bit more dependency injection? Although dependency injection, like every other pattern, shouldn't be used only for the sake of using it, in this case it makes sense to loosely couple the router and its request handlers, and thus making the router really reusable.

This means we need to pass the request handlers from our server into our router, but this feels even more wrong, which is why we should go the whole way and pass them to the server from our main file, and passing it on to the router from there.

How are we going to pass them? Right now we have two handlers, but in a real application, this number is going to increase and vary, and we sure don't want to fiddle around mapping requests to handlers in the router anytime a new URL / request handler is added. And having some *if request == x then call handler y* in the router would be more than ugly.

A varying number of items, each mapped to a string (the requested URL)? Well, sounds like an associative array would be a perfect fit.

Well, this finding is slightly disappointed by the fact that JavaScript doesn't provide associative array - or does it? Turns out, it's actually objects that we want to use if we need an associative array!

There's a nice introduction to this at http://msdn.microsoft.com/en-us/magazine/cc163419.aspx[6], let me quote the relevant part:

> In C++ or C#, when were talking about objects, we're referring to instances of classes or structs. Objects have different properties and methods, depending on which templates (that is, classes) they are instantiated from. That's not the case with JavaScript objects. In JavaScript, objects are just collections of name/value pairs - think of a JavaScript object as a dictionary with string keys.

---

[6]http://msdn.microsoft.com/en-us/magazine/cc163419.aspx

If JavaScript objects are just collections of name/value pairs, how can they have methods? Well, the values can be strings, numbers etc. - or functions!

Ok, now finally back to the code. We decided we want to pass the list of requestHandlers as an object, and in order to achieve loose coupling we want to inject this object into the *route()*.

Let's start with putting the object together in our main file *index.js*:

```
var server = require("./server");
var router = require("./router");
var requestHandlers = require("./requestHandlers");

var handle = {}
handle["/"] = requestHandlers.start;
handle["/start"] = requestHandlers.start;
handle["/upload"] = requestHandlers.upload;

server.start(router.route, handle);
```

Although *handle* is more of a "thing" (a collection of request handlers), I propose we name it like a verb, because this will result in a fluent expression in our router, as we will see soon.

As you can see, it's really simple to map different URLs to the same request handler: by adding a key/value pair of *"/"* and *requestHandlers.start*, we can express in a nice and clean way that not only requests to */start*, but also requests to */* shall be handled by the *start* handler.

After defining our object, we pass it into the server as an additional parameter. Let's change our *server.js* to make use of it:

```
var http = require("http");
var url = require("url");

function start(route, handle) {
```

```
function onRequest(request, response) {
  var pathname = url.parse(request.url).pathname;
  console.log("Request for " + pathname + " received.");

  route(handle, pathname);

  response.writeHead(200, {"Content-Type": "text/plain"});
  response.write("Hello World");
  response.end();
}

http.createServer(onRequest).listen(8888);
console.log("Server has started.");
}

exports.start = start;
```

We've added the *handle* parameter to our *start()* function, and pass the handle object on to the *route()* callback, as its first parameter.

Let's change the *route()* function accordingly, in our *router.js* file:

```
function route(handle, pathname) {
  console.log("About to route a request for " + pathname);
  if (typeof handle[pathname] === 'function') {
    handle[pathname]();
  } else {
    console.log("No request handler found for " + pathname);
  }
}

exports.route = route;
```

What we do here is, we check if a request handler for the given path-name exists, and if it does, we simply call the according function.

Because we can access our request handler functions from our object just as we would access an element of an associative array, we have this nice fluent *handle[pathname]();* expression I talked about earlier: "Please, *handle* this *pathname*".

Ok, that's all we need to wire server, router, and request handlers together! When starting our application and requesting http://localhost:8888/start[7] in our browser, we can prove that the correct request handler was indeed called:

```
Server has started.
Request for /start received.
About to route a request for /start
Request handler 'start' was called.
```

And opening http://localhost:8888/[8] in our browser proves that these requests, too, are indeed handled by the *start* request handler:

```
Request for / received.
About to route a request for /
Request handler 'start' was called.
```

Making the request handlers respond

Beautiful. Now if only the request handlers could actually send something back to the browser, that would be even better, right?

Remember, the "Hello World" your browser displays upon requesting a page still comes from the *onRequest* function in our *server.js* file.

"Handling request" means "answering requests" after all, thus we need to enable our request handlers to speak with the browser just like our *onRequest* function does.

---

[7]http://localhost:8888/start
[8]http://localhost:8888/

How to not do it

The straight-forward approach we - as developers with a background in PHP or Ruby - might want to follow is actually very deceitful: it works like a charm, seems to make a lot of sense, and then suddenly screws things up when we don't expect it.

What I mean by "straight-forward approach" is this: make the request handlers *return()* the content they want to display to the user, and send this response data in the *onRequest* function back to the user.

Let's just do this, and then see why it's not such an overly good idea.

We start with the request handlers and make them return what we would like to display in the browser. We need to change *requestHandlers.js* to this:

```
function start() {
  console.log("Request handler 'start' was called.");
  return "Hello Start";
}

function upload() {
  console.log("Request handler 'upload' was called.");
  return "Hello Upload";
}

exports.start = start;
exports.upload = upload;
```

Good. Likewise, the router needs to return to the server what the request handlers return to him. We therefore need to edit *router.js* like this:

```
function route(handle, pathname) {
  console.log("About to route a request for " + pathname);
```

```
  if (typeof handle[pathname] === 'function') {
    return handle[pathname]();
  } else {
    console.log("No request handler found for " + pathname);
    return "404 Not found";
  }
}

exports.route = route;
```

As you can see, we also return some text if the request could not be routed.

And last but not least, we need to refactor our server to make it respond to the browser with the content the request handlers returned via the router, transforming *server.js* into:

```
var http = require("http");
var url = require("url");

function start(route, handle) {
  function onRequest(request, response) {
    var pathname = url.parse(request.url).pathname;
    console.log("Request for " + pathname + " received.");

    response.writeHead(200, {"Content-Type": "text/plain"});
    var content = route(handle, pathname)
    response.write(content);
    response.end();
  }

  http.createServer(onRequest).listen(8888);
  console.log("Server has started.");
}

exports.start = start;
```

If we start our rewritten application, everything works like a charm: requesting http://localhost:8888/start[9] results in "Hello Start" being displayed in the browser, requesting http://localhost:8888/upload[10] gives us "Hello Upload", and http://localhost:8888/foo[11] produces "404 Not found".

Ok, then why is that a problem? The short answer: because we will run into problems if one the request handlers wants to make use of a non-blocking operation in the future.

Let's take a bit more time for the long answer.

Blocking and non-blocking

As said, the problems will arise when we include non-blocking operations in the request handlers. But let's talk about blocking operations first, then about non-blocking operations.

And instead of trying to explain what "blocking" and "non-blocking" means, let's demonstrate ourselves what happens if we add a blocking operation to our request handlers.

To do this, we will modify our *start* request handler to make it wait 10 seconds before returning its "Hello Start" string. Because there is no such thing as *sleep()* in JavaScript, we will use a clever hack for that.

Please modify *requestHandlers.js* as follows:

```
function start() {
  console.log("Request handler 'start' was called.");

  function sleep(milliSeconds) {
    var startTime = new Date().getTime();
```

---

[9] http://localhost:8888/start
[10] http://localhost:8888/upload
[11] http://localhost:8888/foo

```
    while (new Date().getTime() < startTime + milliSeconds);
  }

  sleep(10000);
  return "Hello Start";
}

function upload() {
  console.log("Request handler 'upload' was called.");
  return "Hello Upload";
}

exports.start = start;
exports.upload = upload;
```

Just to make clear what that does: when the function *start()* is called, Node.js waits 10 seconds and only then returns "Hello Start". When calling *upload()*, it returns immediately, just like before.

(Of course, you should imagine that instead of sleeping for 10 seconds, there would be a real life blocking operation in *start()*, like some sort of long-running computation.)

Let's see what this change does.

As always, we need to restart our server. This time, I ask you to follow a slightly complex "protocol" in order to see what happens: First, open two browser windows or tabs. In the first browser window, please enter http://localhost:8888/start[12] into the address bar, but do not yet open this url!

In the second browser window's address bar, enter http://localhost:8888/upload[13], and again, please do not yet hit enter.

Now, do as follows: hit enter on the first window ("/start"), then quickly change to the second window ("/upload") and hit enter, too.

---

[12] http://localhost:8888/start
[13] http://localhost:8888/upload

What you will notice is this: The /start URL takes 10 seconds to load, as we would expect. But the /upload URL *also* takes 10 seconds to load, although there is no *sleep( )* in the according request handler!

Why? Because *start( )* contains a blocking operation. Like in "it's blocking everything else from working".

And that is a problem, because, as the saying goes: *"In node, everything runs in parallel, except your code".*

What that means is that Node.js can handle a lot of concurrent stuff, but doesn't do this by splitting everything into threads - in fact, Node.js is single-threaded. Instead, it does so by running an event loop, and we the developers can make use of this - we should avoid blocking operations whenever possible, and use non-blocking operations instead.

But to do so, we need to make use of callbacks by passing functions around to other functions that might do something that takes some time (like, e.g. sleep for 10 seconds, or query a database, or do some expensive calculation).

This way we are saying *"Hey, probablyExpensiveFunction( ), please do your stuff, but I, the single Node.js thread, am not going to wait right here until you are finished, I will continue to execute the lines of code below you, so would you please take this callbackFunction( ) here and call it when you are finished doing your expensive stuff? Thanks!"*

(If you would like to read about that in more detail, please have a look at Mixu's post on Understanding the node.js event loop[14].)

And we will now see why the way we constructed the "request handler response handling" in our application doesn't allow us to make proper use of non-blocking operations.

Once again, let's try to experience the problem first-hand by modifying our application.

---

[14]http://blog.mixu.net/2011/02/01/understanding-the-node-js-event-loop/

We are going to use our *start* request handler for this again. Please modify it to reflect the following (file *requestHandlers.js*):

```
var exec = require("child_process").exec;

function start() {
  console.log("Request handler 'start' was called.");
  var content = "empty";

  exec("ls -lah", function (error, stdout, stderr) {
    content = stdout;
  });

  return content;
}

function upload() {
  console.log("Request handler 'upload' was called.");
  return "Hello Upload";
}

exports.start = start;
exports.upload = upload;
```

As you can see, we just introduced a new Node.js module, *child_-process*. We did so because it allows us to make use of a very simple yet useful non-blocking operation: *exec()*.

What *exec()* does is, it executes a shell command from within Node.js. In this example, we are going to use it to get a list of all files in the current directory ("ls -lah"), allowing us to display this list in the browser of a user requesting the */start* URL.

What the code does is straightforward: create a new variable *content* (with an initial value of "empty"), execute "ls -lah", fill the variable with the result, and return it.

As always, we will start our application, and visit http://localhost:8888/start[15].

Which loads a beautiful web page that displays the string "empty". What's going wrong here?

Well, as you may have already guessed, *exec()* does its magic in a non-blocking fashion. That's a good thing, because this way we can execute very expensive shell operations (like, e.g., copying huge files around or similar stuff) without forcing our application into a full stop as the blocking *sleep* operation did.

(If you would like to prove this, replace "ls -lah" with a more expensive operation like "find /").

But we aren't exactly happy with our elegant non-blocking operation, when our browser doesn't display its result, right?

Well, then, let's fix it. And while we are at it, let's try to understand why the current architecture doesn't work.

The problem is that *exec()*, in order to work non-blocking, makes use of a callback function.

In our example, it's an anonymous function which is passed as the second parameter to the *exec()* function call:

```
function (error, stdout, stderr) {
  content = stdout;
}
```

And herein lies the root of our problem: our own code is executed synchronous, which means that immediately after calling *exec()*, Node.js continues to execute *return content;*. At this point, *content* is still "empty", due to the fact that the callback function passed to *exec()* has not yet been called - because *exec()* operates asynchronous.

Now, "ls -lah" is a very inexpensive and fast operation (unless there are millions of files in the directory). Which is why the callback

---

[15]http://localhost:8888/start

is called relatively expeditious - but it nevertheless happens asynchronously.

Thinking about a more expensive command makes this more obvious: "find /" takes about 1 minute on my machine, but if I replace "ls -lah" with "find /" in the request handler, I still immediately receive an HTTP response when opening the /start URL - it's clear that *exec()* does something in the background, while Node.js itself continues with the application, and we may assume that the callback function we passed into *exec()* will be called only when the "find /" command has finished running.

But how can we achieve our goal, i.e. showing the user a list of files in the current directory?

Well, after learning how to *not* do it, let's discuss how to make our request handlers respond to browser requests the right way.

Responding request handlers with non-blocking operations

I've just used the phrase "the right way". Dangerous stuff. Quite often, there is no single "right way".

But one possible solution for this is, as often with Node.js, to pass functions around. Let's examine this.

Right now, our application is able to transport the content (which the request handlers would like to display to the user) from the request handlers to the HTTP server by returning it up through the layers of the application (request handler -> router -> server).

Our new approach is as follows: instead of bringing the content to the server, we will bring the server to the content. To be more precise, we will inject the *response* object (from our server's callback function *onRequest()*) through the router into the request handlers. The handlers will then be able to use this object's functions to respond to requests themselves.

Enough explanation, here is the step by step recipe on how to change our application.

Let's start with our *server.js*:

```
var http = require("http");
var url = require("url");

function start(route, handle) {
  function onRequest(request, response) {
    var pathname = url.parse(request.url).pathname;
    console.log("Request for " + pathname + " received.");

    route(handle, pathname, response);
  }

  http.createServer(onRequest).listen(8888);
  console.log("Server has started.");
}

exports.start = start;
```

Instead of expecting a return value from the *route()* function, we pass it a third parameter, our *response* object. Furthermore, we removed any *response* method calls from the *onRequest()* handler, because we now expect *route* to take care of that.

Next comes *router.js*:

```
function route(handle, pathname, response) {
  console.log("About to route a request for " + pathname);
  if (typeof handle[pathname] === 'function') {
    handle[pathname](response);
  } else {
    console.log("No request handler found for " + pathname);
    response.writeHead(404, {"Content-Type": "text/plain"});
```

```
    response.write("404 Not found");
    response.end();
  }
}
```

```
exports.route = route;
```

Same pattern: instead of expecting a return value from our request handlers, we pass the *respond* object on.

If no request handler can be used, we now take care of responding with a proper "404" header and body ourselves.

And last but not least, we modify *requestHandlers.js*:

```
var exec = require("child_process").exec;

function start(response) {
  console.log("Request handler 'start' was called.");

  exec("ls -lah", function (error, stdout, stderr) {
    response.writeHead(200, {"Content-Type": "text/plain"});
    response.write(stdout);
    response.end();
  });
}

function upload(response) {
  console.log("Request handler 'upload' was called.");
  response.writeHead(200, {"Content-Type": "text/plain"});
  response.write("Hello Upload");
  response.end();
}

exports.start = start;
exports.upload = upload;
```

Our handler functions need to accept the response parameter, and have to make use of them in order to respond to the request directly.

The *start* handler will respond from within the anonymous *exec()* callback, and the *upload* handler still simply replies with "Hello Upload", but now by making use of the *response* object.

If we start our application again (*node index.js*), this should work as expected.

If you would like to prove that an expensive operation behind */start* will no longer block requests for */upload* from answering immediately, then modify your *requestHandlers.js* as follows:

```
var exec = require("child_process").exec;

function start(response) {
  console.log("Request handler 'start' was called.");

  exec("find /",
    { timeout: 10000, maxBuffer: 20000*1024 },
    function (error, stdout, stderr) {
      response.writeHead(200, {"Content-Type": "text/plain"});
      response.write(stdout);
      response.end();
    });
}

function upload(response) {
  console.log("Request handler 'upload' was called.");
  response.writeHead(200, {"Content-Type": "text/plain"});
  response.write("Hello Upload");
  response.end();
}

exports.start = start;
exports.upload = upload;
```

This will make HTTP requests to http://localhost:8888/start[16] take at least 10 seconds, but requests to http://localhost:8888/upload[17] will be answered immediately, even if /start is still computing.

Serving something useful

Until now, what we have done is all fine and dandy, but we haven't created any value for the customers of our award-winning website.

Our server, router, and request handlers are in place, thus now we can begin to add content to our site which allows our users to interact and walk through the use case of choosing a file, uploading this file, and viewing the uploaded file in the browser. For the sake of simplicity we will assume that only image files are going to be uploaded and displayed through the application.

Ok, let's take it step by step, but with most of the techniques and principles of JavaScript explained by now, let's at the same time accelerate a bit. This author likes to hear himself talking way too much anyways.

Here, step by step means roughly two steps: We will first look at how to handle incoming POST requests (but not file uploads), and in a second step, we will make use of an external Node.js module for the file upload handling. I've chosen this approach for two reasons.

First, handling basic POST requests is relatively simple with Node.js, but still teaches us enough to be worth exercising it. Second, handling file uploads (i.e., multipart POST requests) is *not* simple with Node.js, and therefore is beyond the scope of this tutorial, but using an external module is itself a lesson that makes sense to be included in a beginner's tutorial.

---

[16]http://localhost:8888/start
[17]http://localhost:8888/upload

Handling POST requests

Let's keep this banally simple: We will present a textarea that can be filled by the user and submitted to the server in a POST request. Upon receiving and handling this request, we will display the content of the textarea.

The HTML for this textarea form needs to be served by our */start* request handler, so let's add it right away, in file *requestHandlers.js*:

```
function start(response) {
  console.log("Request handler 'start' was called.");

  var body = '<html>'+
    '<head>'+
    '<meta http-equiv="Content-Type" content="text/html; '+
    'charset=UTF-8" />'+
    '</head>'+
    '<body>'+
    '<form action="/upload" method="post">'+
    '<textarea name="text" rows="20" cols="60"></textarea>'+
    '<input type="submit" value="Submit text" />'+
    '</form>'+
    '</body>'+
    '</html>';

    response.writeHead(200, {"Content-Type": "text/html"});
    response.write(body);
    response.end();
}

function upload(response) {
  console.log("Request handler 'upload' was called.");
  response.writeHead(200, {"Content-Type": "text/plain"});
  response.write("Hello Upload");
  response.end();
```

```
}
```

```
exports.start = start;
exports.upload = upload;
```

Now if this isn't going to win the Webby Awards, then I don't know what could. You should see this very simple form when requesting http://localhost:8888/start[18] in your browser. If not, you probably didn't restart the application.

I hear you: having view content right in the request handler is ugly. However, I decided to not include that extra level of abstraction (i.e., separating view and controller logic) in this tutorial, because I think that it doesn't teach us anything worth knowing in the context of JavaScript or Node.js.

Let's rather use the remaining screen space for a more interesting problem, that is, handling the POST request that will hit our */upload* request handler when the user submits this form.

Now that we are becoming expert novices, we are no longer surprised by the fact that handling POST data is done in a non-blocking fashion, by using asynchronous callbacks.

Which makes sense, because POST requests can potentially be very large - nothing stops the user from entering text that is multiple megabytes in size. Handling the whole bulk of data in one go would result in a blocking operation.

To make the whole process non-blocking, Node.js serves our code the POST data in small chunks, callbacks that are called upon certain events. These events are *data* (an new chunk of POST data arrives) and *end* (all chunks have been received).

We need to tell Node.js which functions to call back to when these events occur. This is done by adding *listeners* to the *request* object

---

[18]http://localhost:8888/start

that is passed to our *onRequest* callback whenever an HTTP request is received.

This basically looks like this:

```
request.addListener("data", function(chunk) {
  // called when a new chunk of data was received
});

request.addListener("end", function() {
  // called when all chunks of data have been received
});
```

The question arises where to implement this logic. We currently can access the *request* object in our server only - we don't pass it on to the router and the request handlers, like we did with the *response* object.

In my opinion, it's an HTTP servers job to give the application all the data from a requests it needs to do its job. Therefore, I suggest we handle the POST data processing right in the server and pass the final data on to the router and the request handlers, which then can decide what to do with it.

Thus, the idea is to put the *data* and *end* event callbacks in the server, collecting all POST data chunks in the *data* callback, and calling the router upon receiving the *end* event, while passing the collected data chunks on to the router, which in turn passes it on to the request handlers.

Here we go, starting with *server.js*:

```
var http = require("http");
var url = require("url");

function start(route, handle) {
  function onRequest(request, response) {
    var postData = "";
```

```
    var pathname = url.parse(request.url).pathname;
    console.log("Request for " + pathname + " received.");

    request.setEncoding("utf8");

    request.addListener("data", function(postDataChunk) {
      postData += postDataChunk;
      console.log("Received POST data chunk '"+
      postDataChunk + "'.");
    });

    request.addListener("end", function() {
      route(handle, pathname, response, postData);
    });

  }

  http.createServer(onRequest).listen(8888);
  console.log("Server has started.");
}

exports.start = start;
```

We basically did three things here: First, we defined that we expect
the encoding of the received data to be UTF-8, we added an event
listener for the "data" event which step by step fills our new *postData*
variable whenever a new chunk of POST data arrives, and we moved
the call to our router into the *end* event callback to make sure it's only
called when all POST data is gathered. We also pass the POST data
into the router, because we are going to need it in our request handlers.

Adding the console logging on every chunk that is received probably
is a bad idea for production code (megabytes of POST data, remember?), but makes sense to see what happens.

I suggest playing around with this a bit. Put small amounts of text into the textarea as well as lots of text, and you will see that for the larger texts, the *data* callback is indeed called multiple times.

Let's add even more awesome to our app. On the /upload page, we will display the received content. To make this possible, we need to pass the *postData* on to the request handlers, in *router.js*:

```
function route(handle, pathname, response, postData) {
  console.log("About to route a request for " + pathname);
  if (typeof handle[pathname] === 'function') {
    handle[pathname](response, postData);
  } else {
    console.log("No request handler found for " + pathname);
    response.writeHead(404, {"Content-Type": "text/plain"});
    response.write("404 Not found");
    response.end();
  }
}

exports.route = route;
```

And in *requestHandlers.js*, we include the data in our response of the *upload* request handler:

```
function start(response, postData) {
  console.log("Request handler 'start' was called.");

  var body = '<html>'+
    '<head>'+
    '<meta http-equiv="Content-Type" content="text/html; '+
    'charset=UTF-8" />'+
    '</head>'+
    '<body>'+
    '<form action="/upload" method="post">'+
    '<textarea name="text" rows="20" cols="60"></textarea>'+
```

```
     '<input type="submit" value="Submit text" />'+
     '</form>'+
     '</body>'+
     '</html>';

     response.writeHead(200, {"Content-Type": "text/html"});
     response.write(body);
     response.end();
}

function upload(response, postData) {
  console.log("Request handler 'upload' was called.");
  response.writeHead(200, {"Content-Type": "text/plain"});
  response.write("You've sent: " + postData);
  response.end();
}

exports.start = start;
exports.upload = upload;
```

That's it, we are now able to receive POST data and use it in our request handlers.

One last thing for this topic: what we pass on to the router and the request handlers is the complete body of our POST request. We will probably want to consume the individual fields that make up the POST data, in this case, the value of the *text* field.

We already read about the *querystring* module, which assists us with this:

```
var querystring = require("querystring");

function start(response, postData) {
  console.log("Request handler 'start' was called.");
```

```
  var body = '<html>'+
    '<head>'+
    '<meta http-equiv="Content-Type" content="text/html; '+
    'charset=UTF-8" />'+
    '</head>'+
    '<body>'+
    '<form action="/upload" method="post">'+
    '<textarea name="text" rows="20" cols="60"></textarea>'+
    '<input type="submit" value="Submit text" />'+
    '</form>'+
    '</body>'+
    '</html>';

    response.writeHead(200, {"Content-Type": "text/html"});
    response.write(body);
    response.end();
}

function upload(response, postData) {
  console.log("Request handler 'upload' was called.");
  response.writeHead(200, {"Content-Type": "text/plain"});
  response.write("You've sent the text: "+
  querystring.parse(postData).text);
  response.end();
}

exports.start = start;
exports.upload = upload;
```

Well, for a beginner's tutorial, that's all there is to say about handling POST data.

Handling file uploads

Let's tackle our final use case. Our plan was to allow users to upload an image file, and display the uploaded image in the browser.

Back in the 90's this would have qualified as a business model for an IPO, today it must suffice to teach us two things: how to install external Node.js libraries, and how to make use of them in our own code.

The external module we are going to use is *node-formidable* by Felix Geisendoerfer. It nicely abstracts away all the nasty details of parsing incoming file data. At the end of the day, handling incoming files is "only" about handling POST data - but the devil really *is* in the details here, and using a ready-made solution makes a lot of sense in this case.

In order to make use of Felix' code, the according Node.js module needs to be installed. Node.js ships with its own package manager, dubbed *NPM*. It allows us to install external Node.js modules in a very convenient fashion. Given a working Node.js installation, it boils down to issuing

```
npm install formidable
```

on our command line. If the following output ends with

```
npm info build Success: formidable@1.0.2
npm ok
```

then we are good to go.

The *formidable* module is now available to our own code - all we need to do is requiring it just like one of the built-in modules we used earlier:

```
var formidable = require("formidable");
```

The metaphor formidable uses is that of a form being submitted via HTTP POST, making it parseable in Node.js. All we need to do is create a new *IncomingForm*, which is an abstraction of this submitted form, and which can then be used to parse the *request* object of our HTTP server for the fields and files that were submitted through this form.

The example code from the node-formidable project page shows how the different parts play together:

```
var formidable = require('formidable'),
    http = require('http'),
    sys = require('sys');

http.createServer(function(req, res) {
  if (req.url == '/upload' && req.method.toLowerCase() == 'post') {
    // parse a file upload
    var form = new formidable.IncomingForm();
    form.parse(req, function(err, fields, files) {
      res.writeHead(200, {'content-type': 'text/plain'});
      res.write('received upload:\n\n');
      res.end(sys.inspect({fields: fields, files: files}));
    });
    return;
  }

  // show a file upload form
  res.writeHead(200, {'content-type': 'text/html'});
  res.end(
    '<form action="/upload" enctype="multipart/form-data" '+
    'method="post">'+
    '<input type="text" name="title"><br>'+
    '<input type="file" name="upload" multiple="multiple"><br>'+
    '<input type="submit" value="Upload">'+
    '</form>'
  );
```

```
}).listen(8888);
```

If we put this code into a file and execute it through *node*, we are able to submit a simple form, including a file upload, and see how the *files* object, which is passed to the callback defined in the *form.parse* call, is structured:

```
received upload:
```

```
{ fields: { title: 'Hello World' },
  files:
   { upload:
      { size: 1558,
        path: '/tmp/1c747974a27a6292743669e91f29350b',
        name: 'us-flag.png',
        type: 'image/png',
        lastModifiedDate: Tue, 21 Jun 2011 07:02:41 GMT,
        _writeStream: [Object],
        length: [Getter],
        filename: [Getter],
        mime: [Getter] } } }
```

In order to make our use case happen, what we need to do is to include the form-parsing logic of formidable into our code structure, plus we will need to find out how to serve the content of the uploaded file (which is saved into the */tmp* folder) to a requesting browser.

Let's tackle the latter one first: if there is an image file on our local hardrive, how do we serve it to a requesting browser?

We are obviously going to read the contents of this file into our Node.js server, and unsurprisingly, there is a module for that - it's called *fs*.

Let's add another request handler for the URL */show*, which will hard-codingly display the contents of the file */tmp/test.png*. It of course makes a lot of sense to save a real png image file to this location first.

We are going to modify *requestHandlers.js* as follows:

```
var querystring = require("querystring"),
    fs = require("fs");

function start(response, postData) {
  console.log("Request handler 'start' was called.");

  var body = '<html>'+
    '<head>'+
    '<meta http-equiv="Content-Type" '+
    'content="text/html; charset=UTF-8" />'+
    '</head>'+
    '<body>'+
    '<form action="/upload" method="post">'+
    '<textarea name="text" rows="20" cols="60"></textarea>'+
    '<input type="submit" value="Submit text" />'+
    '</form>'+
    '</body>'+
    '</html>';

    response.writeHead(200, {"Content-Type": "text/html"});
    response.write(body);
    response.end();
}

function upload(response, postData) {
  console.log("Request handler 'upload' was called.");
  response.writeHead(200, {"Content-Type": "text/plain"});
  response.write("You've sent the text: "+
  querystring.parse(postData).text);
  response.end();
}

function show(response, postData) {
  console.log("Request handler 'show' was called.");
  fs.readFile("/tmp/test.png", "binary", function(error, file) {
```

```
    if(error) {
      response.writeHead(500, {"Content-Type": "text/plain"});
      response.write(err + "\n");
      response.end();
    } else {
      response.writeHead(200, {"Content-Type": "image/png"});
      response.write(file, "binary");
      response.end();
    }
  });
}

exports.start = start;
exports.upload = upload;
exports.show = show;
```

We also need to map this new request handler to the URL */show* in file *index.js*:

```
var server = require("./server");
var router = require("./router");
var requestHandlers = require("./requestHandlers");

var handle = {}
handle["/"] = requestHandlers.start;
handle["/start"] = requestHandlers.start;
handle["/upload"] = requestHandlers.upload;
handle["/show"] = requestHandlers.show;

server.start(router.route, handle);
```

By restarting the server and opening http://localhost:8888/show[19] in the browser, the image file saved at */tmp/test.png* should be displayed.

Fine. All we need to do now is

---

[19] http://localhost:8888/show

- add a file upload element to the form which is served at */start*,

- integrate node-formidable into the *upload* request handler, in order to save the uploaded file to */tmp/test.png*,

- embed the uploaded image into the HTML output of the */upload* URL.

Step 1 is simple. We need to add an encoding type of *multipart/form-data* to our HTML form, remove the textarea, add a file upload input field, and change the submit button text to "Upload file". Let's do just that in file *requestHandlers.js*:

```
var querystring = require("querystring"),
    fs = require("fs");

function start(response, postData) {
  console.log("Request handler 'start' was called.");

  var body = '<html>'+
    '<head>'+
    '<meta http-equiv="Content-Type" '+
    'content="text/html; charset=UTF-8" />'+
    '</head>'+
    '<body>'+
    '<form action="/upload" enctype="multipart/form-data" '+
    'method="post">'+
    '<input type="file" name="upload">'+
    '<input type="submit" value="Upload file" />'+
    '</form>'+
    '</body>'+
    '</html>';

  response.writeHead(200, {"Content-Type": "text/html"});
  response.write(body);
  response.end();
```

```
}

function upload(response, postData) {
  console.log("Request handler 'upload' was called.");
  response.writeHead(200, {"Content-Type": "text/plain"});
  response.write("You've sent the text: "+
  querystring.parse(postData).text);
  response.end();
}

function show(response, postData) {
  console.log("Request handler 'show' was called.");
  fs.readFile("/tmp/test.png", "binary", function(error, file) {
    if(error) {
      response.writeHead(500, {"Content-Type": "text/plain"});
      response.write(err + "\n");
      response.end();
    } else {
      response.writeHead(200, {"Content-Type": "image/png"});
      response.write(file, "binary");
      response.end();
    }
  });
}

exports.start = start;
exports.upload = upload;
exports.show = show;
```

Great. The next step is a bit more complex of course. The first problem is: we want to handle the file upload in our *upload* request handler, and there, we will need to pass the *request* object to the *form.parse* call of node-formidable.

But all we have is the *response* object and the *postData* array. Sad panda. Looks like we will have to pass the *request* object all the way from the server to the router to the request handler. There may be more elegant solutions, but this approach should do the job for now.

And while we are at it, let's remove the whole *postData* stuff in our server and request handlers - we won't need it for handling the file upload, and it even raises a problem: we already "consumed" the *data* events of the *request* object in the server, which means that *form.parse*, which also needs to consume those events, wouldn't receive any more data from them (because Node.js doesn't buffer any data).

Let's start with *server.js* - we remove the postData handling and the *request.setEncoding* line (which is going to be handled by node-formidable itself), and we pass *request* to the router instead:

```
var http = require("http");
var url = require("url");

function start(route, handle) {
  function onRequest(request, response) {
    var pathname = url.parse(request.url).pathname;
    console.log("Request for " + pathname + " received.");
    route(handle, pathname, response, request);
  }

  http.createServer(onRequest).listen(8888);
  console.log("Server has started.");
}

exports.start = start;
```

Next comes *router.js* - we don't need to pass *postData* on anymore, and instead pass *request*:

```
function route(handle, pathname, response, request) {
  console.log("About to route a request for " + pathname);
```

```
    if (typeof handle[pathname] === 'function') {
      handle[pathname](response, request);
    } else {
      console.log("No request handler found for " + pathname);
      response.writeHead(404, {"Content-Type": "text/html"});
      response.write("404 Not found");
      response.end();
    }
  }
}

exports.route = route;
```

Now, the *request* object can be used in our *upload* request handler function. node-formidable will handle the details of saving the uploaded file to a local file within */tmp*, but we need to make sure that this file is renamed to */tmp/test.png* ourselves. Yes, we keep things really simple and assume that only PNG images will be uploaded.

For now, *fs.renameSync(path1, path2)* will do the job. Beware! As the name implies, it works synchronous, thus if the rename operation should be expensive and take a long time, it will lead to blocking. Let's just agree that we are all grown-ups here and know what we are doing.

Let's put the pieces of managing the uploaded file and renaming it together now, in file *requestHandlers.js*:

```
var querystring = require("querystring"),
    fs = require("fs"),
    formidable = require("formidable");

function start(response) {
  console.log("Request handler 'start' was called.");

  var body = '<html>' +
    '<head>' +
```

```
      '<meta http-equiv="Content-Type" content="text/html; '+
      'charset=UTF-8" />'+
      '</head>'+
      '<body>'+
      '<form action="/upload" enctype="multipart/form-data" '+
      'method="post">'+
      '<input type="file" name="upload" multiple="multiple">'+
      '<input type="submit" value="Upload file" />'+
      '</form>'+
      '</body>'+
      '</html>';

      response.writeHead(200, {"Content-Type": "text/html"});
      response.write(body);
      response.end();
}

function upload(response, request) {
  console.log("Request handler 'upload' was called.");

  var form = new formidable.IncomingForm();
  console.log("about to parse");
  form.parse(request, function(err, fields, files) {
    console.log("parsing done");
    fs.renameSync(files.upload.path, "/tmp/test.png");
    response.writeHead(200, {"Content-Type": "text/html"});
    response.write("received image:<br/>");
    response.write("<img src='/show' />");
    response.end();
  });
}

function show(response) {
  console.log("Request handler 'show' was called.");
  fs.readFile("/tmp/test.png", "binary", function(error, file) {
```

```
    if(error) {
      response.writeHead(500, {"Content-Type": "text/plain"});
      response.write(err + "\n");
      response.end();
    } else {
      response.writeHead(200, {"Content-Type": "image/png"});
      response.write(file, "binary");
      response.end();
    }
  });
}

exports.start = start;
exports.upload = upload;
exports.show = show;
```

And that's it. Restart the server, and the complete use case will be available. Select a local PNG image from your hardrive, upload it to the server, and have it displayed in the web page.

Conclusion and outlook

Congratulations, our mission is accomplished! We wrote a simple yet full-fledged Node.js web application. We talked about server-side JavaScript, functional programming, blocking and non-blocking operations, callbacks, events, custom, internal and external modules, and a lot more.

Of course, there's a lot of stuff we did not talk about: how to talk to a database, how to write unit tests, how to create external modules that are installable via NPM, or even something simple like how to handle GET requests.

But that's the fate of every book aimed at beginners - it can't talk about every single aspect in every single detail.

The good news is, the Node.js community is extremly vibrant (think of an ADHD kid on caffeine, but in a positive way), which means there are a lot of resources out there, and a lot of places to get your questions answered. The Node.js community wiki[1] and the Node-Cloud directory[2] are probably the best starting points for more information.

---

[1] https://github.com/joyent/node/wiki
[2] http://www.nodecloud.org/